LETTER TO THE READER

Dear Reader,

 Congratulations! Simply having this book in your hands could be the beginning of your journey to a healthier life.

 I have been a medical doctor since 1991, however over the last few years I have noticed that diseases that were once only seen in adults are now affecting young children. If this trend continues, then children are destined to die young, even before their parents. So, as a doctor and a mom, I have asked my three children to join me in writing this book for you.

 This book is to empower children like yourself to adopt a healthier lifestyle and thus control your health destiny. Only you have the power to change the future of our healthcare crisis.

 In this book you will find some basic principles for good health. I know that change is never easy. However, someone rightly said, "The journey of a million miles begins with the first step", so don't be afraid to begin. We want you to read this book carefully, do your best to practice what you learn, then share the knowledge with your parents, teachers, family, and friends.

 Please keep this thought always in mind, that you have the power to control your health destiny so go out and do it.

 And we will see you at the corner of Amazing Health Avenue and Longevity Lane!

We love you all.
Dr. Cooper and the Kidz

Charlie goes to the Doctor™
3604 N. McColl Road
McAllen, TX 78501
www.cooperwellnesscenter.com

Medical Disclaimer:

Every effort has been made to ensure that the information contained in this book is complete and accurate. However, the ideas, procedures, and suggestions contained herein are not intended as a substitute for consulting with your physician. This book is intended to educate, inspire, and empower you to make lifestyle changes that will propel to a healthier, happier, and more fulfilled life. You should use information received in this book wisely, always consult with your primary healthcare provider if you have questions or concerns. The information received in this book should be used to supplement not to replace medical advice from your primary healthcare provider.

Neither the author nor the publisher shall be liable or responsible for any loss or damage allegedly arising from any information or suggestion in this book. Further, while every effort has been made to provide accurate contact information and Internet addresses at the time of publication, neither the author nor the publisher assumes any responsibility for errors, or for changes that occur after publication.

Edited by Alison Green
Illustrated and Designed by Edgardo Gonzalez
Contributors for activities: Melrose Dockery and Yolande Dockery

ISBN: 978-0-9973379-4-5

Manufactured in the United States of America

Charlie Goes to the Doctor

Written by
Dona Cooper-Dockery M.D.

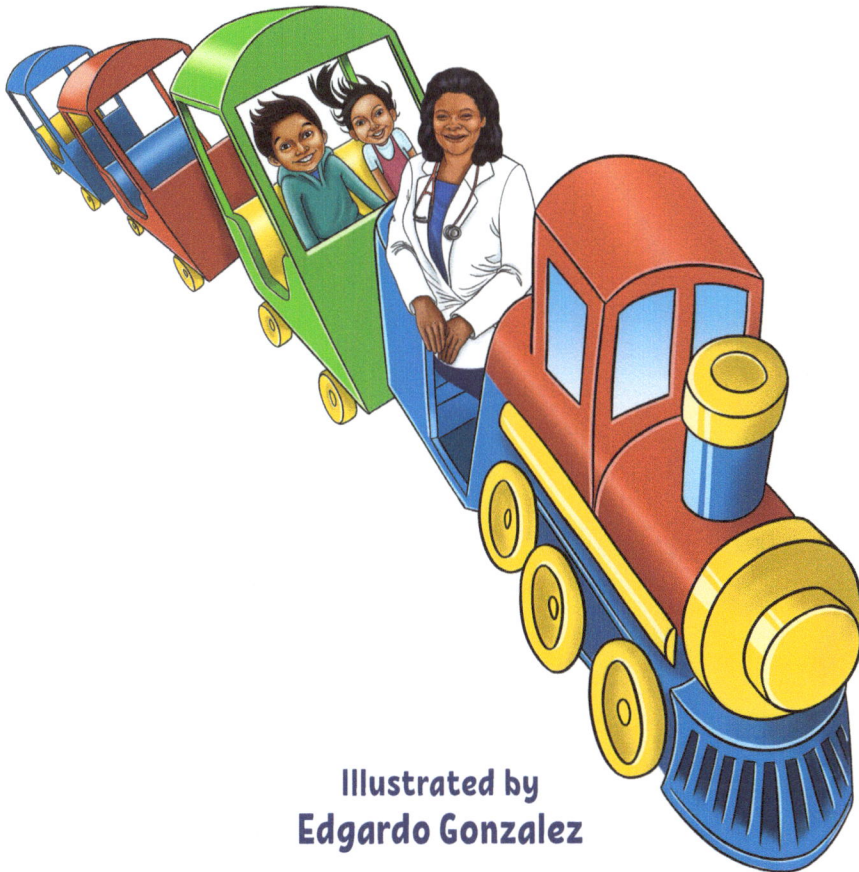

Illustrated by
Edgardo Gonzalez

AAAHCHOO!!!

"Mom, mom, I'm not feeling so well," said Charlie.

"Hi, Charlie, Charlie, you don't look so well. What's the matter?" asked Charlie's mom.

"Mom, I have a sore throat and my ear aches and my tummy aches. I don't feel well. I don't want to go to school today," said Charlie.

"Hey, Charlie, let me check. You don't look well at all. Why don't I take you to Doctor C and let her evaluate your condition?" asked Charlie's mom.

3

"Good morning, Dr. Cooper," said Charlie.

"Hi, Charlie. What's the matter with you? You don't look yourself today," said Dr. Cooper.

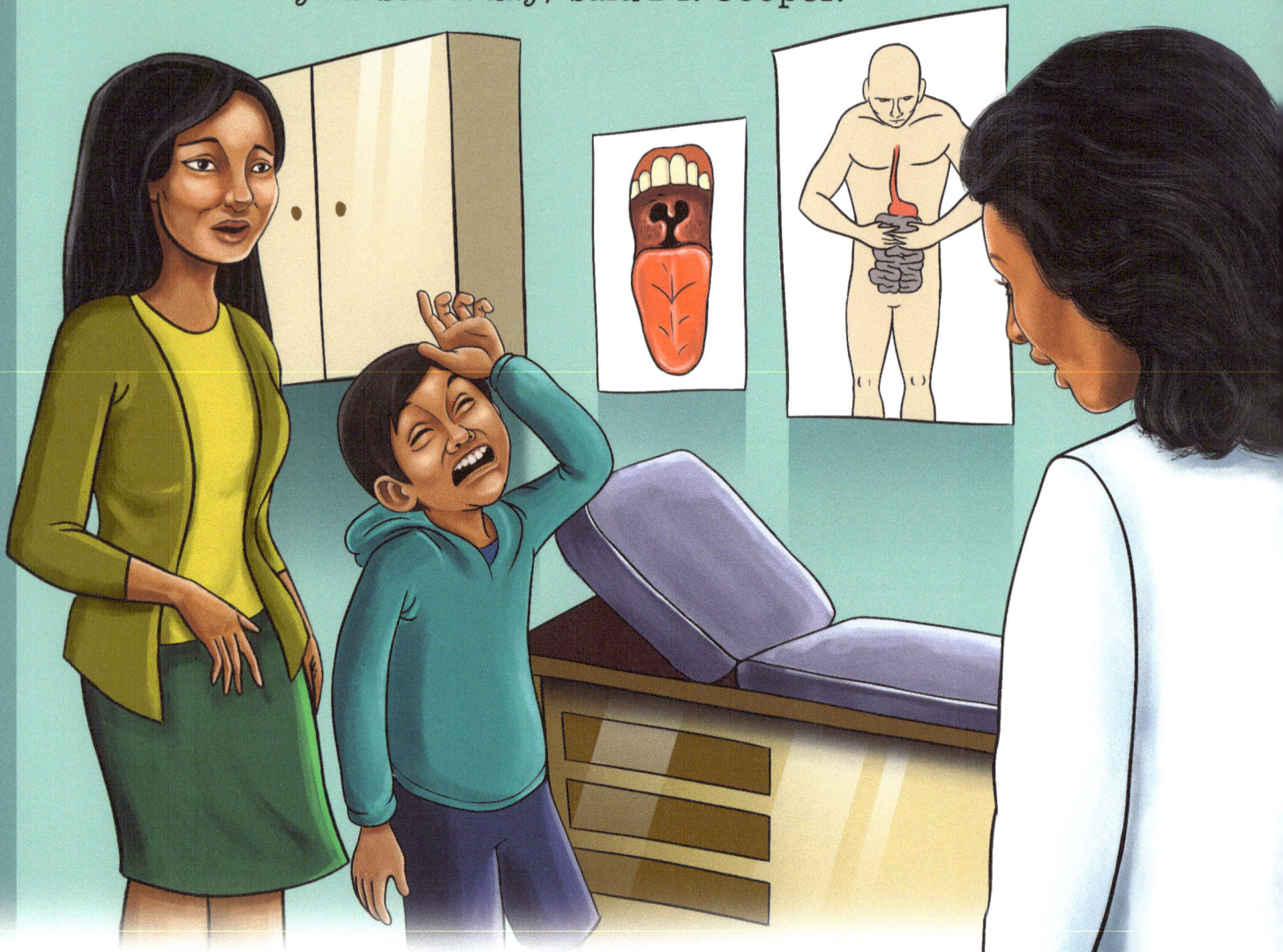

"Hey, Dr. Cooper, I don't feel well. I have a headache, I'm coughing and my tummy ... I feel like I'm going to die. Please help me, Dr. Cooper, I really don't want to die so young!" said Charlie.

"Hey, Charlie. No, you're not going to die. What would you like me to do for you today?" asked Dr. Cooper.

4

"Dr. Cooper, I want to feel well. I want this pain to go away and the cough to stop. I want to feel well, I want to live a long and healthy life," said Charlie.

"You know what, I think I can help you. Okay, Charlie, let's get you up on the exam table. I'm going to check and see what's wrong," said Dr. Cooper.

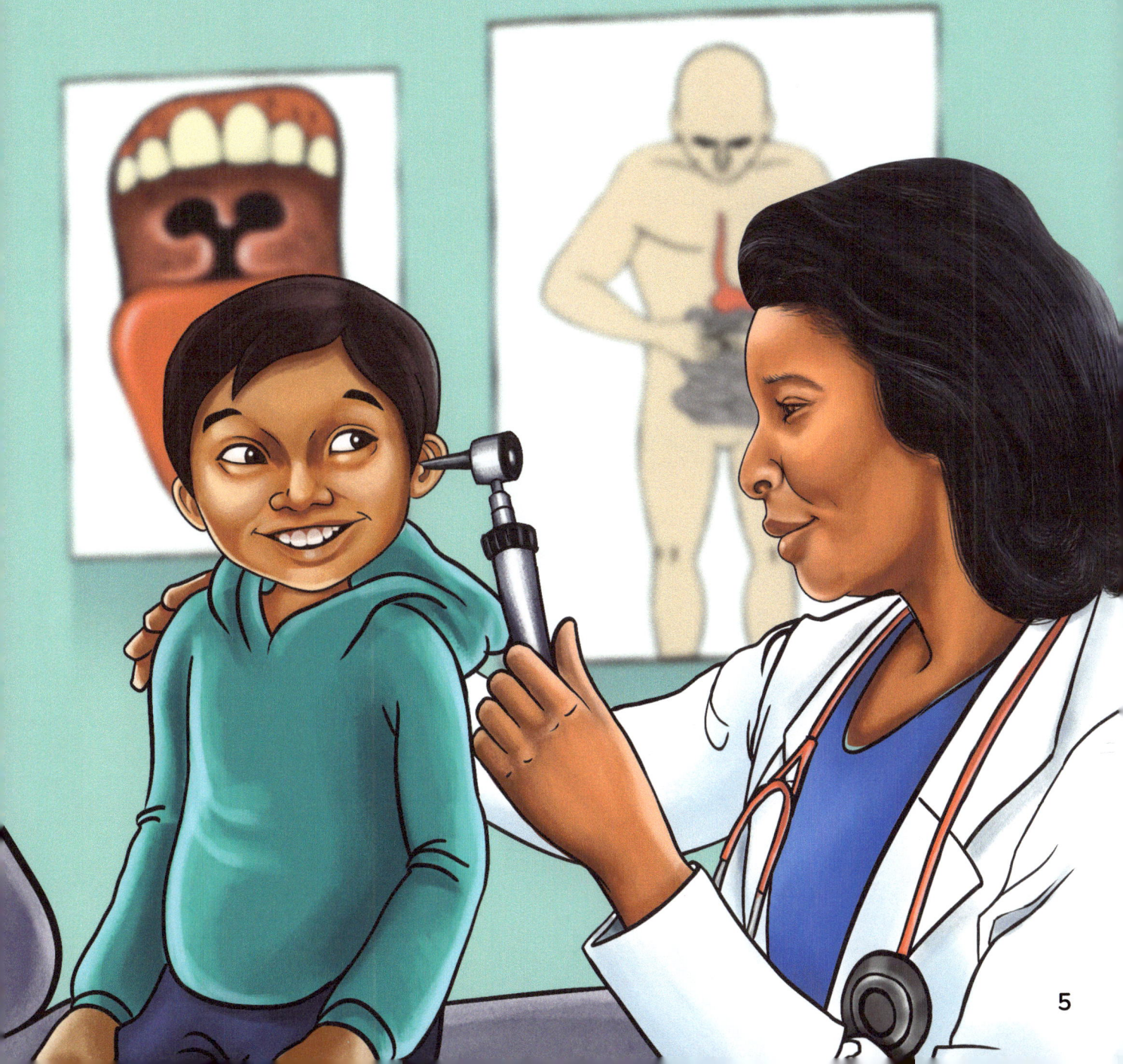

"There is no need to worry. Well, I see two large red tonsils and there's fluid behind the left eardrum. Now it's time to see what's happening with your tummy," said Dr. Cooper.

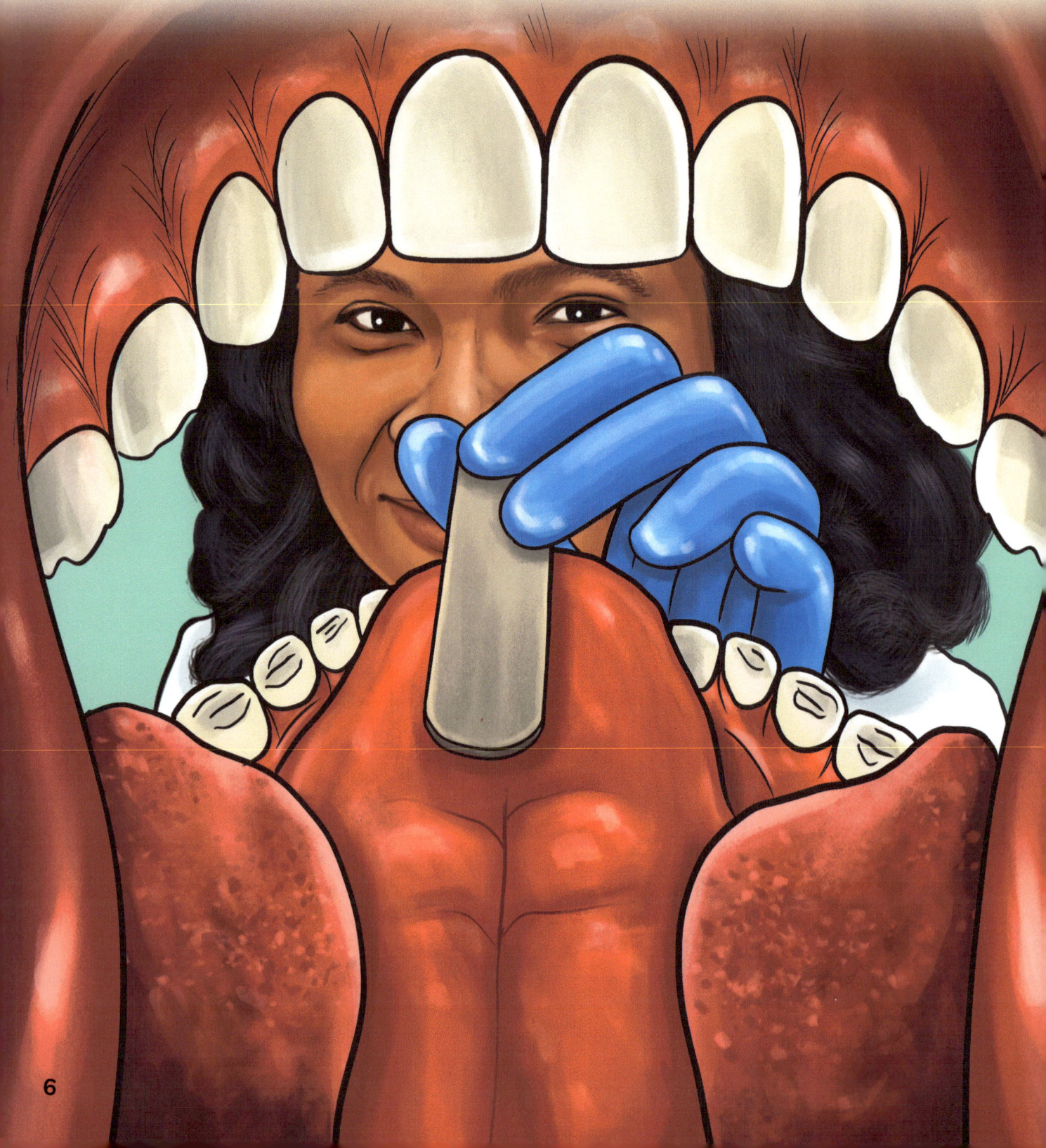

"Ouch! Ouch! That hurts Dr. Cooper," said Charlie.

"I'm sorry, Charlie, I never meant to hurt you, but now I see the problem. You have a bad case of pharyngitis with mesenteric adenitis," said Dr. Cooper.

"Pharyngiiiitis , meseeeennnteric adenitis? What's that? (Charlie starts crying.) Does this mean that I'm going to die, Dr. Cooper?" asked Charlie.

"Oh no, Charlie, pharyngitis is just a fancy doctor's term for an infection of the throat or tonsils. And mesenteric adenitis is indicating that your body's defense system is now in action to fight the infection," said Dr. Cooper.

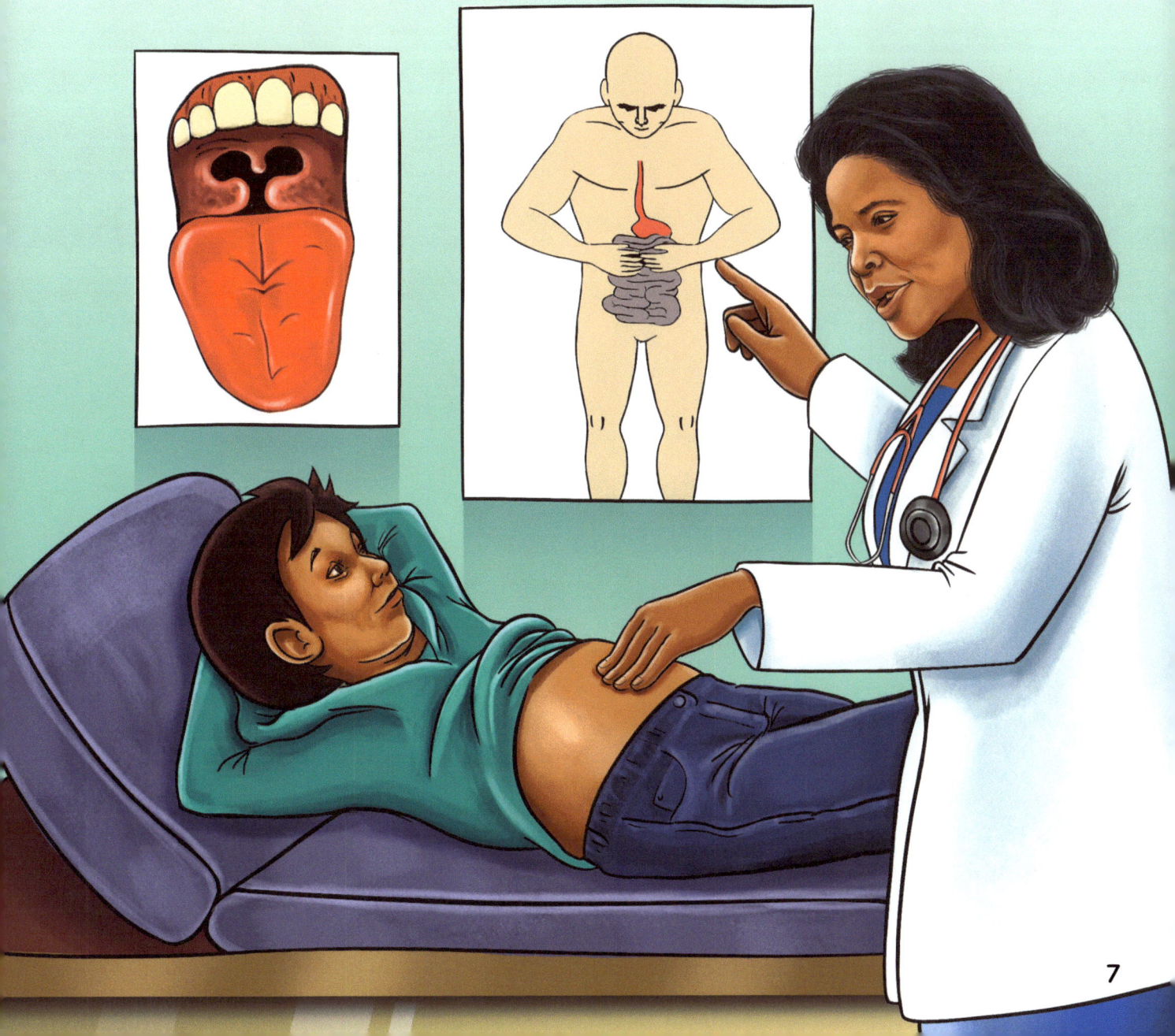

"Really, Dr. Cooper! So I'm not actually dying and my body can turn on some good soldiers to protect me when I'm sick?" said Charlie.

"Yep, Charlie, you're so smart. It didn't take you so long to understand the concept. By the way, you're looking better. Hey, Charlie, I'd love to take you on a journey and show how to keep sickness away, so that you can enjoy a happier, healthier and more energetic life," said Dr. Cooper.

"I'm ready, let's do it!" said Charlie.

"Then let's hop on the train! We're on our way
to the land of amazing health and happiness.
Toot! Toot! All aboard!!" said Dr. Cooper.

"Yippee! Let's go!" said Charlie.

"Welcome to the GET HEALTHY train. We're on our way to the land of amazing health where people live for a long time. On this excursion you'll learn how to take care of your body and keep the bad boy, Sick Ness, away," said Dr. Cooper.

"Wow! I'm so excited, I want to visit the land of amazing health! I want to live for a long time," said Charlie.

"Our first stop is Station G where G is for Goals. Here you're encouraged to think of your situation and what you want your health to be like. Ask yourself, Do I want to feel tired at times? Do I want to have tummy pain or a cough? Or do I want to feel healthy and strong?" said Dr. Cooper.

"Yes! I know! I know! I want to feel healthy and strong all the time," said Charlie.

"Then you must think positively, believe in yourself, set your goals and take action to win. You may have some difficulty at times, but quitting should not be an option. Remember to ask for help from someone like mom, dad, or a good friend," said Dr. Cooper.

"Great, Dr. Cooper. My goal today is to stop this pain in my throat and my ear and get to school so I can learn how to change the world and make it a better place," said Charlie.

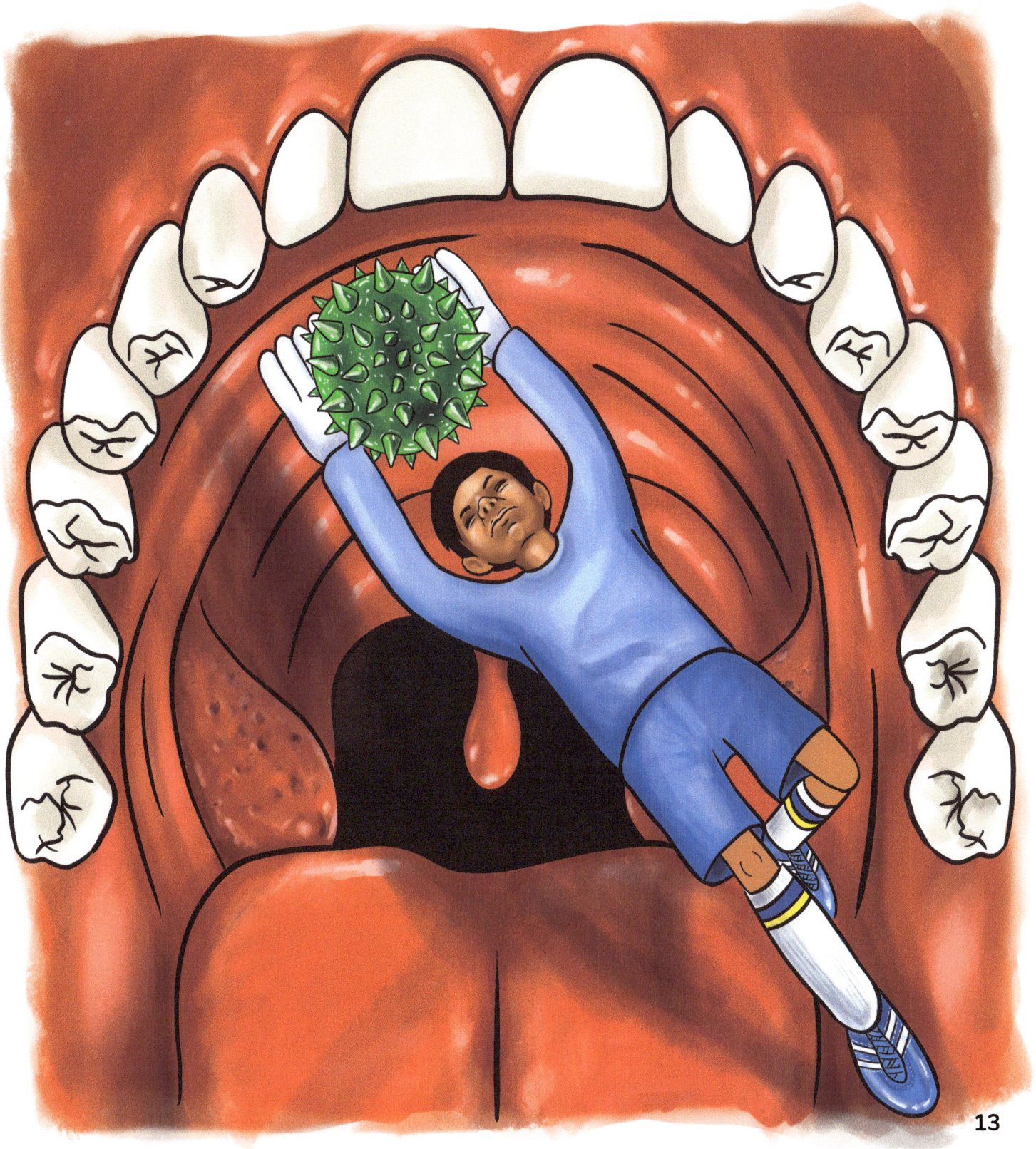

"Hello everyone. We're now at Station E where E is for Environment. Let's get off the train and enjoy this beautiful place," said Dr. Cooper.

"Hey, Charlie! I'm Darling Sunshine. If you spend 10 minutes daily with me, your body will produce enough vitamin D to keep your bones healthy and strong," said Darling Sunshine.

"Hey, Charlie! I'm Serotonin, the happy hormone. I'll keep you smiling and happy, but you need Darling Sunshine for me to function at my best," said, Serotonin.

"Hey, Sunshine, why do some people block you when they go outdoors?" said Charlie.

"Well, well, that's a very smart question, Charlie. Too much exposure to my B rays could cause skin cancer. Remember, you only need to hang out with me 10 minutes daily, and the best time to do so is between 10 am and 3 pm.," said Darling Sunshine.

"Move over, Mr. Sunshine, here comes the one and only Mr. Fresh Air. Charlie, let me tell you, here in the E zone, I'm your guy! I have Oxygen with me and you need him to stay alive, so you need to breathe deep and fill up your lungs with fresh air. This will keep your cells healthy and you'll feel more energetic and stronger," said Mr. Fresh Air.

"Now let's hop over to Station T where T is for Timely Rest. Charlie, I know that you're very excited to have met Darling Sunshine and Mr. Fresh Air, and that you even got a boost of happiness from Serotonin, but now is the time to relax and rest. Let's talk a little about that. Are you getting enough sleep at night?" asked Dr. Cooper.

"Oh, Dr. Cooper, not really. Sometimes I go to bed very late because I spend lots of time watching TV or playing video games," said Charlie.

"You know, Charlie, it's so important for you to get enough rest at night. You see, your body needs time to repair and heal any damaged cells or tissues and this happens at night when you're resting. During sleep at night, certain hormones for growth, appetite and stress are at work with the one goal to keep you healthy. During sleep your brain will organize information learnt during the day in your long-term memory, so if you want to be smart, you need to get adequate sleep at night," said Dr. Cooper.

"Wow! That's awesome, I didn't know that when I sleep at night, my body is working to fix my damaged cells and preserve my memory. I want to be smart and healthy! So how much sleep do I need?" asked Charlie.

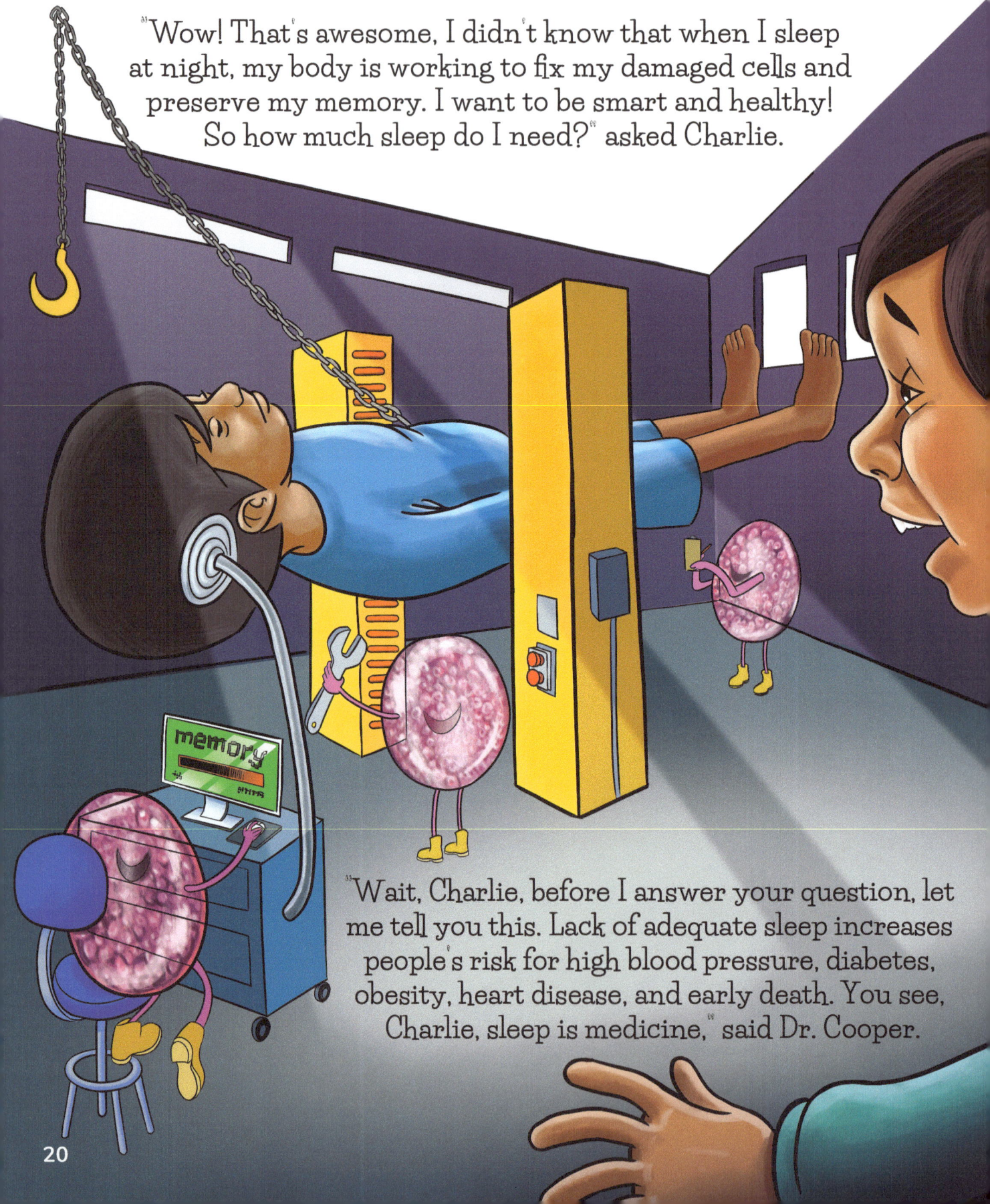

"Wait, Charlie, before I answer your question, let me tell you this. Lack of adequate sleep increases people's risk for high blood pressure, diabetes, obesity, heart disease, and early death. You see, Charlie, sleep is medicine," said Dr. Cooper.

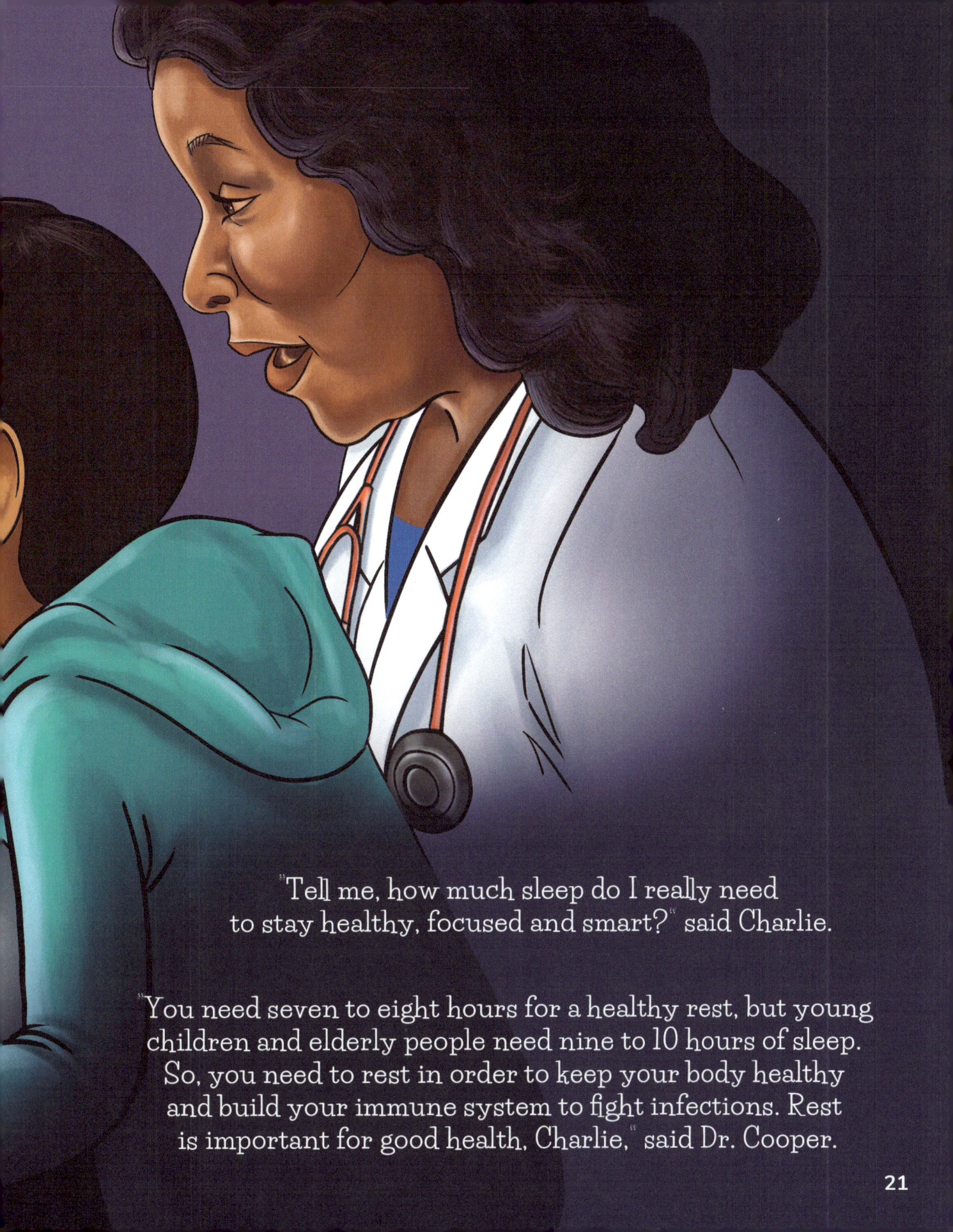

"Tell me, how much sleep do I really need
to stay healthy, focused and smart?" said Charlie.

"You need seven to eight hours for a healthy rest, but young
children and elderly people need nine to 10 hours of sleep.
So, you need to rest in order to keep your body healthy
and build your immune system to fight infections. Rest
is important for good health, Charlie," said Dr. Cooper.

"Now on to Station H where H is for Healthy Nutrition. There, we'll be taking a long walk through Greenville where you'll meet many of my wonderful friends. So, Charlie, let's hop over to Greenville," said Dr. Cooper.

"Hey, hey, Charlie, Charlie! Hey, hey, I'm Mrs. Kale! I'm the Queen of Greenville and if you eat me, you're going to live a long time because you're going to have plenty of vitamin A, vitamin C and calcium. Calcium helps growing children build strong bones and it's found in foods other than cow's milk like me," said Mrs. Kale.

"Hey, Charlie. Hey. Charlie, I am Mr. Broccoli. I'm the King of Greenville. Eat me and you get a lot of protein, fiber, and vitamins K and C that are all good for health. You're going to feel better. Did you know, Charlie, that vitamin C helps the body heal cuts and wounds? So the next time you get a scrape or cut, remember to eat foods full of vitamin C," said Mr. Broccoli.

"Hey, Charlie, hey! I'm Mr. Carrot. You see? I'm so orange. I have a lot of beautiful chemicals, beta carotenoid and vitamin A to give you good vision and to keep your cells strong and healthy," said Mr. Carrot.

"Hey, Charlie, Charlie! I'm over here. I'm Mr. Beet. You can see how red and strong I am. I also have a lot of iron and folate, which are great to keep your blood healthy. I also have lots of vitamin A, and potassium. Eat me and I'll help to increase your levels of nitric oxide, a chemical that dilates your blood vessels and thus lowers your blood pressure. Eat me and keep your heart super healthy!" said Mr. Beet.

"Hey, Charlie, Charlie, Charlie! Hey, look over here! I'm Mrs. Orange. You see, I have a lot of vitamin C and I could hear you coughing. You eat me and you're going to feel better. The cough is going to improve and your immune system will be strengthened. Eat me! I am so good for you," said Mrs. Orange.

"Hey, Charlie, Charlie! I'm Mr. Sweet Potato. If you want some good quality energy, as well as the ability to see well in the dark, then eat me! I'm a nutritious carbohydrate filled with iron, calcium, many different B vitamins and vitamin A that you need for good health," said Mr. Sweet Potato.

"Hey, Charlie! Hey, hey, Charlie! Come over here! I'm Grandma Legume. Let me introduce you to a few of my family members. We have Kidney Bean, Pinto Bean, Lima Bean, Lentil, Chickpea and Black Bean. Some people call us the poor man's meat, but we have lots of protein, and best of all we have no cholesterol to clog up your arteries. Eat us to build strong muscles and bones and we'll also keep your heart healthy and pumping. We also have lots of fiber and healthy carbohydrates. We're great for people with diabetes because we don't elevate the blood sugar."

"Hey, come over here. How could I forget my little son, Peanut? Some people think he's a nut but he's actually a legume. Kids like to eat him in peanut butter and jelly sandwiches. Hey, Charlie, don't be afraid to eat us and we'll help you live a long life," said Grandma Legume.

"Hey, Charlie, Charlie! Come on over here and meet the Berry Quartet! I'm Blueberry, this is Strawberry, Raspberry and Grape. We're filled with vitamins and antioxidant which keep your cells healthy. Antioxidants help protect your body against free radicals that can harm your DNA and cause cell death. A portion of berries a day can help you live longer, so eat us!" said Blueberry.

"Hey, hey, Charlie, look up here! I'm your friend Banana. I'm succulent and delicious and filled with potassium, folate, healthy sugar, and vitamin B. Some people like to use me in ice cream and smoothies. Eat me and you'll become healthier and happier," said Banana.

"Hello, look over here! I'm Miss Apple. I'm beautiful and round, and you can find me in green, yellow or red. Some people say that if you eat me once a day, you'll keep Dr. Cooper away forever. So eat me and you'll get lots of vitamin C, fiber and many nutrients that will keep you well for a long time," said Miss Apple.

"Hey, Charlie! Charlie, hey! I'm a healthy whole grain and my name is Quinoa. Meet my brother and sister, Brown Rice and Oats. Have you heard of us? We're healthy carbohydrates and we're also filled with proteins, vitamins, iron, minerals, and fiber. You can enjoy us in sweet and savory dishes. Sometimes we're processed and stripped of our fiber and nutrients, so please ask mom to purchase brown rice, rolled oats or oat groats. Tell her to avoid white rice and white flour because those aren't so nutritious," said Quinoa.

"Charlie, Charlie! Come over here meet the nut bunch – Walnut, Cashew, Pecan, Almond, and the others. They have good fats, fiber, protein, and vitamins. You only need to eat a handful of nuts a day to be healthy," said Dr. Cooper.

"Hey, Dr. Cooper, I want to get out of Greenville. I'm starting to get hungry and I want to go home to ask mom to prepare some of those delicious fruits, vegetables and grains that I met in Greenville. Hey wait, Dr. Cooper, look over there! I see lots of food that I like to eat with my friends; I see Pizza, Hot Dog, Chips, Soda, Candy and much more. What area is that?" asked Charlie.

"Charlie, that area is called Danger Junction. If you take that path you'll get to famous O. B. City. There you'll meet Major Sick Ness and his friends, Diabetes, Heart Disease, Mr. Hyper Tension, and the others. Those people aren't nice and I really want to keep you away from them. So let's stay away from Danger junction with those processed foods. You really don't want to go to O. B. City," said Dr. Cooper.

"Okay, Dr. Cooper, let's move on to the next stop. Station A is for Access to Healthcare, so what will I learn there? Oh! I see a lot of needles over here. I'm afraid!" said Charlie.

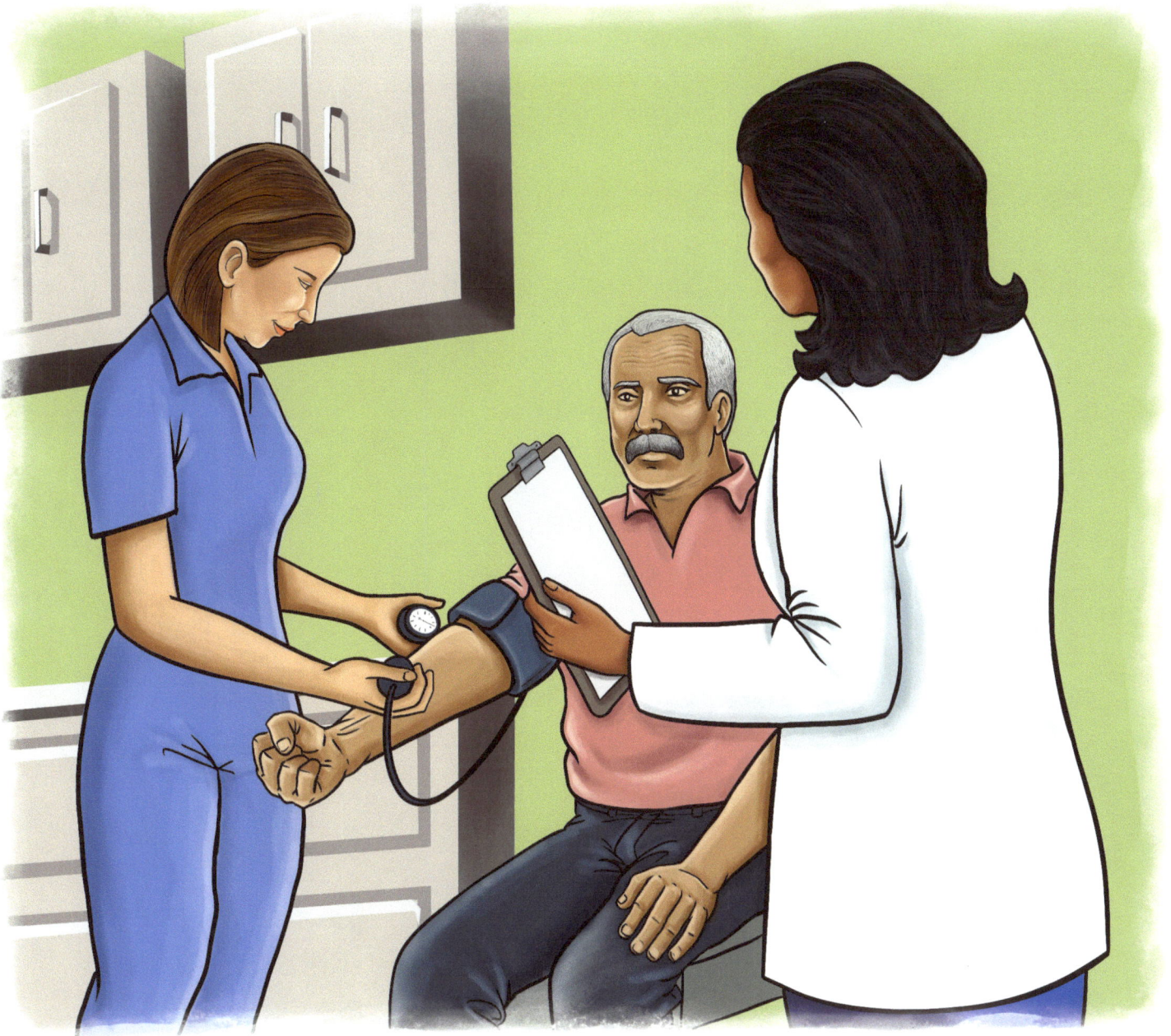

"No need to be afraid. At this station I want you to learn some basic information. Charlie, most people should go to see their healthcare provider at least once per year and during that visit they should ask for basic information such as their blood pressure reading and their blood sugar and cholesterol levels. They should also discuss topics such as vaccinations and the various healthcare screening tests that they may need depending on their age and risk factors. Charlie, this information is all that you need at this station today," said Dr. Cooper.

"Dr. Cooper, does this mean I won't be getting a shot today?" asked Charlie.

"Yes, Charlie. Doctors don't always give shots, so don't be afraid when mom or dad needs to take you to the doctor's office," said Dr. Cooper.

"Oh, Dr. Cooper, I want to get out of here. I still don't like needles," said Charlie.

"All right, Charlie, let's move along," said Dr. Cooper.

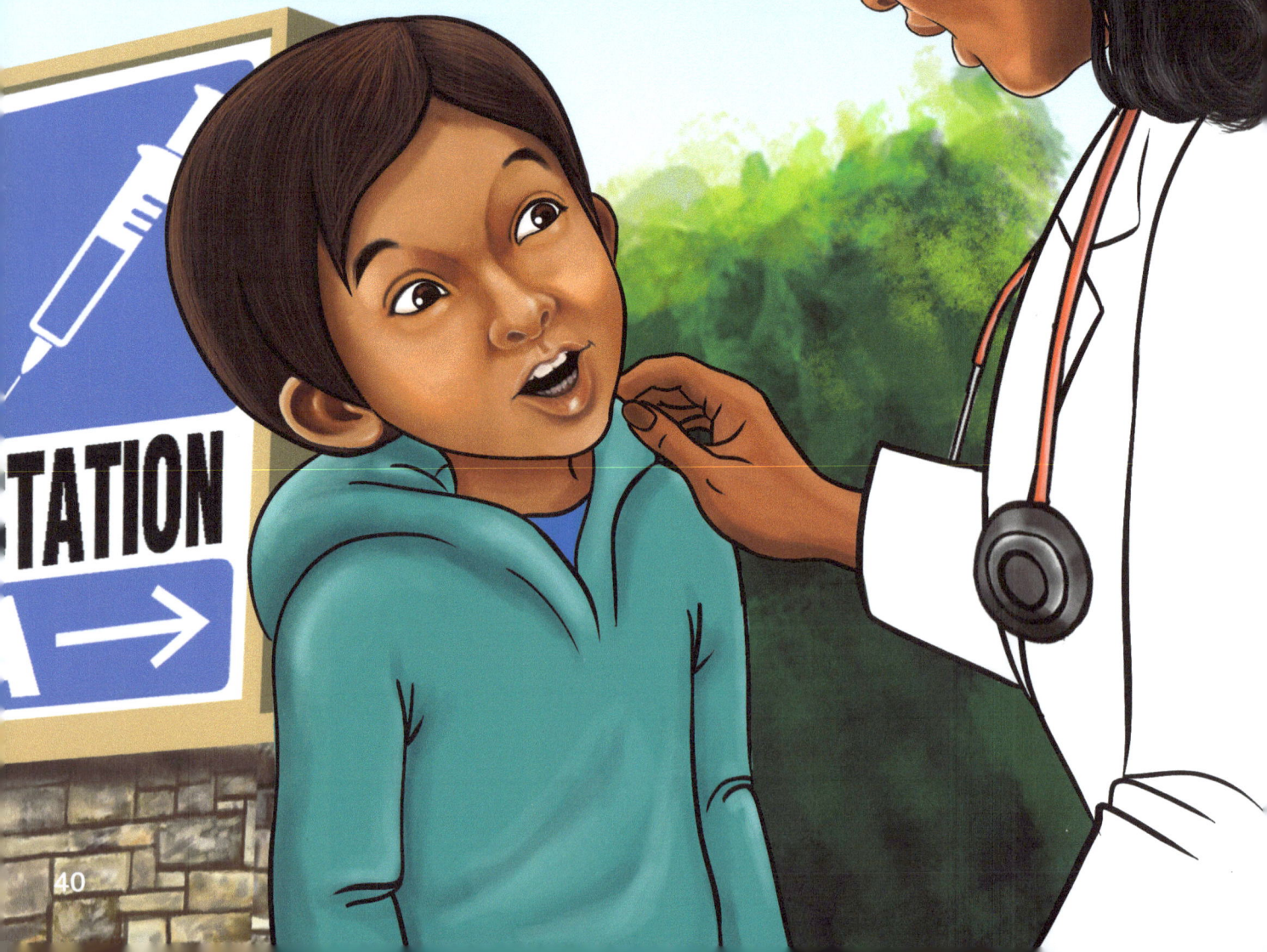

"Oh, Dr. Cooper, I'm so tired and thirsty. What do you have here to drink?" asked Charlie..

"Let's go over here to Station L which stands for Liquid. Let's go see what we have to drink. Charlie, do you like to drink water?" asked Dr. Cooper.

"I like sugary drinks like soda," said Charlie.

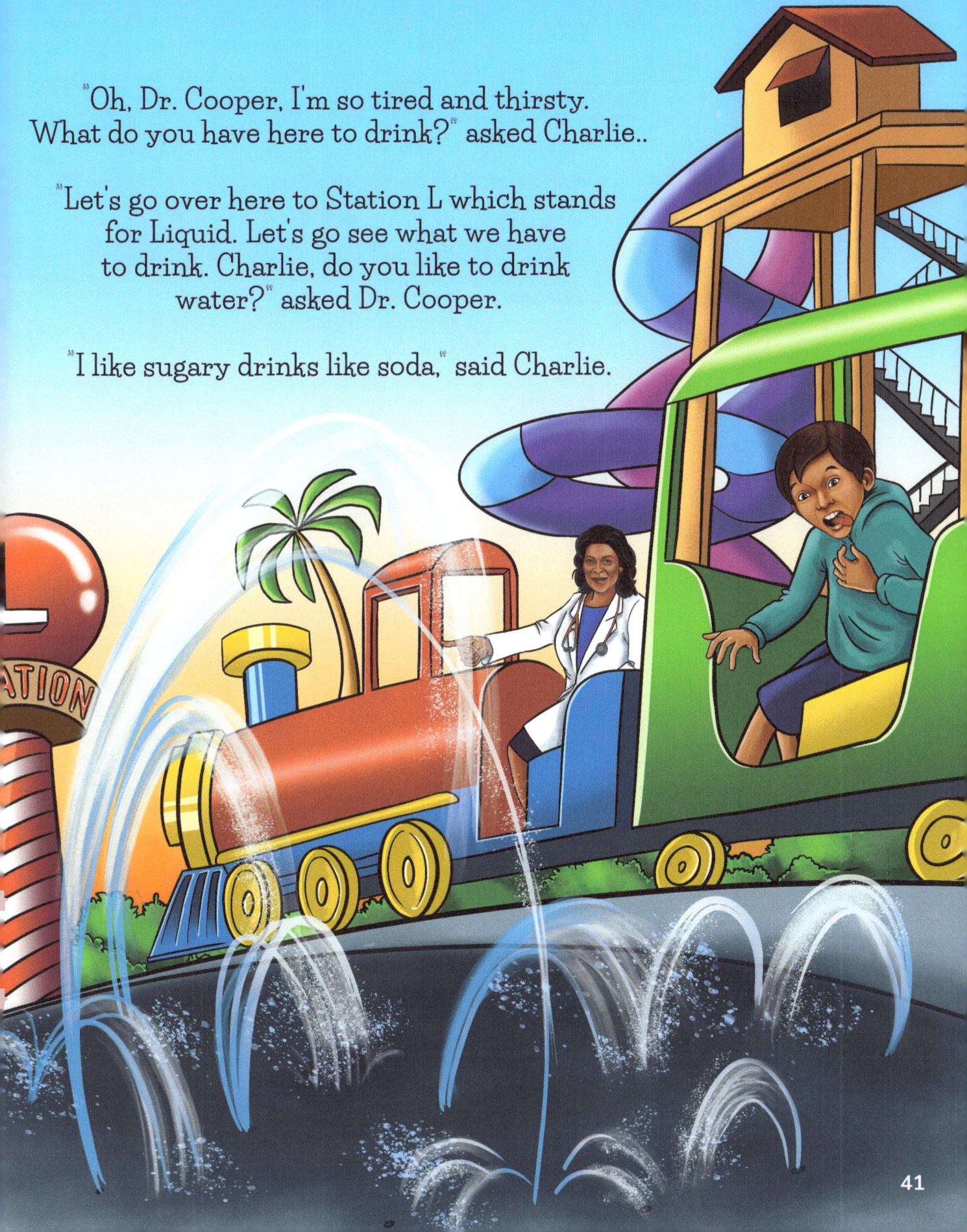

"You know, Charlie, those sugary drinks have a lot of sugar. For example, one can of soda contains 15 teaspoons of sugar. That's a lot of sugar and it's not good for your health. You need to ask mom to give you clean and fresh water. You need to drink enough water for your size," said Dr. Cooper.

One bottle of soda = 15 teaspoons of sugar

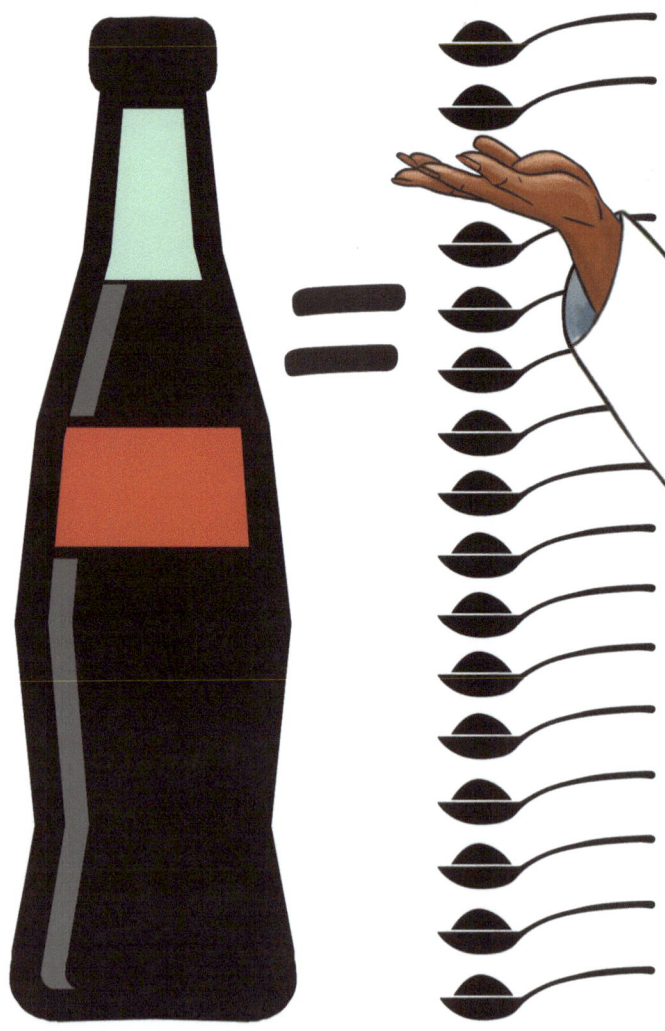

"Mom could also sometimes give you freshly made organic fruit or vegetable juice, because these are filled with vitamins and minerals. But you must stay away from sodas and sweet concentrated juices," said Dr. Cooper.

"Charlie, did you know that your body is mostly water?" asked Dr. Cooper.

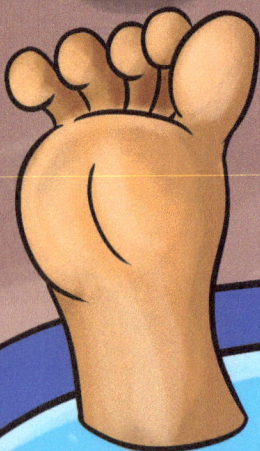

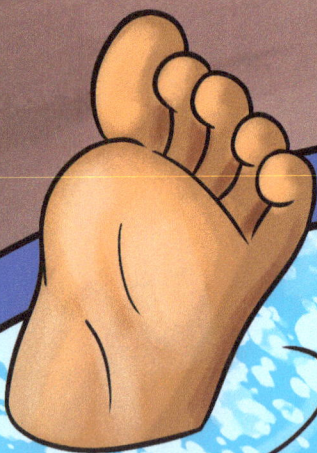

"Are you sure, Dr. Cooper? I'm mostly water?" asked Charlie.

"Yes, Charlie. You're about 70% of water, and you need to keep yourself really hydrated because lack of water can cause you to feel tired, give you headaches or constipation, and lead to confusion and many other health problems. So, drinking water is good for your health. You need to stay away from lots of sugar," said Dr. Cooper.

"Hey, Charlie, let's walk over there to Station T.
T is for Time with Family and Friends.
Who is that little girl over there?
She looks lonely and so sad.
Hello, what's your name?" asked Dr. Cooper

"I'm Annie and I'm alone. My friends all left me
and I'm feeling sad," said Annie.

"Come along with us! Let's play a game!" said Charlie.

"Why don't you two hug? You know, friendship is good for your health because as you spend time together and learn more about each other, you can strengthen each other in times of need and that's wonderful for good health. Why don't you run along and become friends? Remember to be kind to those around you. Don't say hurtful things but treat others as you would want to be treated. If someone tries to hurt you, please share that information with your parents, teacher or an adult you really trust," said Dr. Cooper.

"All right, Dr. Cooper. We will!" said Charlie.

"Well, I see that you're both having fun, so let's move on to Station H. H is for Happiness. I see that you're both looking happier now than when you met. Did you also know that happiness is good medicine?" said Dr. Cooper.

"You know, guys, let me tell you a story. A long, long time ago, a wise man Solomon wrote in the Good Old Book that a merry heart is good medicine, but a broken spirit dries the bones."

"So, when you're happy, your body produces happy hormones which allow you to feel well. They can lower your blood pressure, lower your blood sugar, and protect you from many illnesses. So remember to keep a happy song in your heart always."

"Guess what? We forgot to go over to station E. E is for Exercise at EXO City," said Dr. Cooper.

"EXO City? What's that, Dr. Cooper?" asked Charlie.

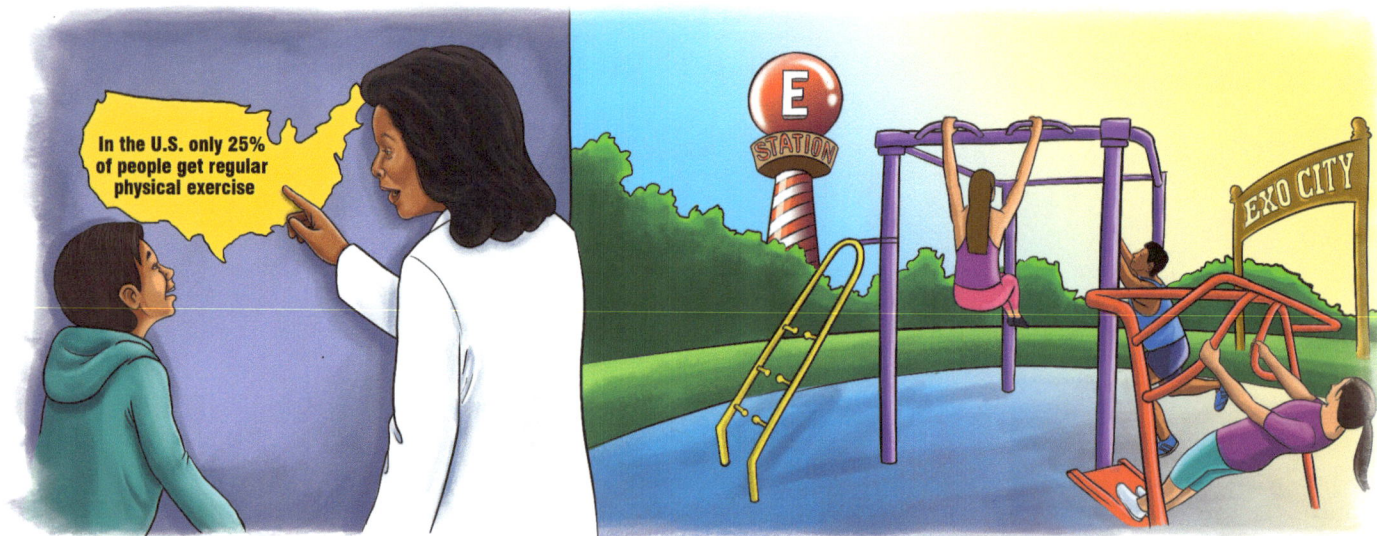

In the U.S. only 25% of people get regular physical exercise

"Charlie, in the United States only 25% of people get regular physical exercise. Exercise is medicine because many diseases can be prevented or improved with exercise. So let's go over to EXO City where we're going to meet Mr. Muscle Man," said Dr. Cooper.

"Hi, Charlie and Annie. I'm Mr. Muscle Man. I can make you feel strong, energetic, and healthy." said Mr. Muscle Man.

"Let's talk numbers. Children under 18 need to spend SIXTY minutes a day doing physical activities such as running, walking, playing sports, swimming, bicycling, or any other activities that you enjoy. Sitting at the TV screen, computer, iPad or cell phone for long periods of time is not good for your health," said Mr. Muscle Man.

"Mr. Muscle Man, I'd like to have a body like yours. What do I need to do?" said Charlie.

"Okay, Charlie and Annie, let's work out. March, children, steadily round the school and always remember Mr. Muscle Man's rule: Heads up and footsteps firm aligned, hands behind, shoulders back and face, be bright. Move forward: forward march, forward, forward, forward march. Backward: backward, move backward, backward march, backward. To the left, to the left, to the left, to the left, to the left. Stamp your feet: one, two, three, four, five. Then repeat: stamp your feet, one, two, three, four, five. Then to the right, to the right, to the right, to the right, to the right," said Mr. Muscle Man.

"Clap your hands: one, two, three, four, five. Repeat!
Clap your hands: one, two, three, four, five. Now march forward,
forward, forward! Move forward, forward! Stamp your feet: one, two,
three, four, five. Then repeat: one, two, three, four, five. Now to the left,
to the left, to the left, to the left, to the left.
Clap your hands: one, two, three, four, five. And repeat: one, two, three,
four, five. Jumping Jacks: one, two, three, four, five. Repeat: one, two,
three, four, five. And now sit down!" said Mr. Muscle Man.

"Wow, what a workout! I feel great!" said Charlie.

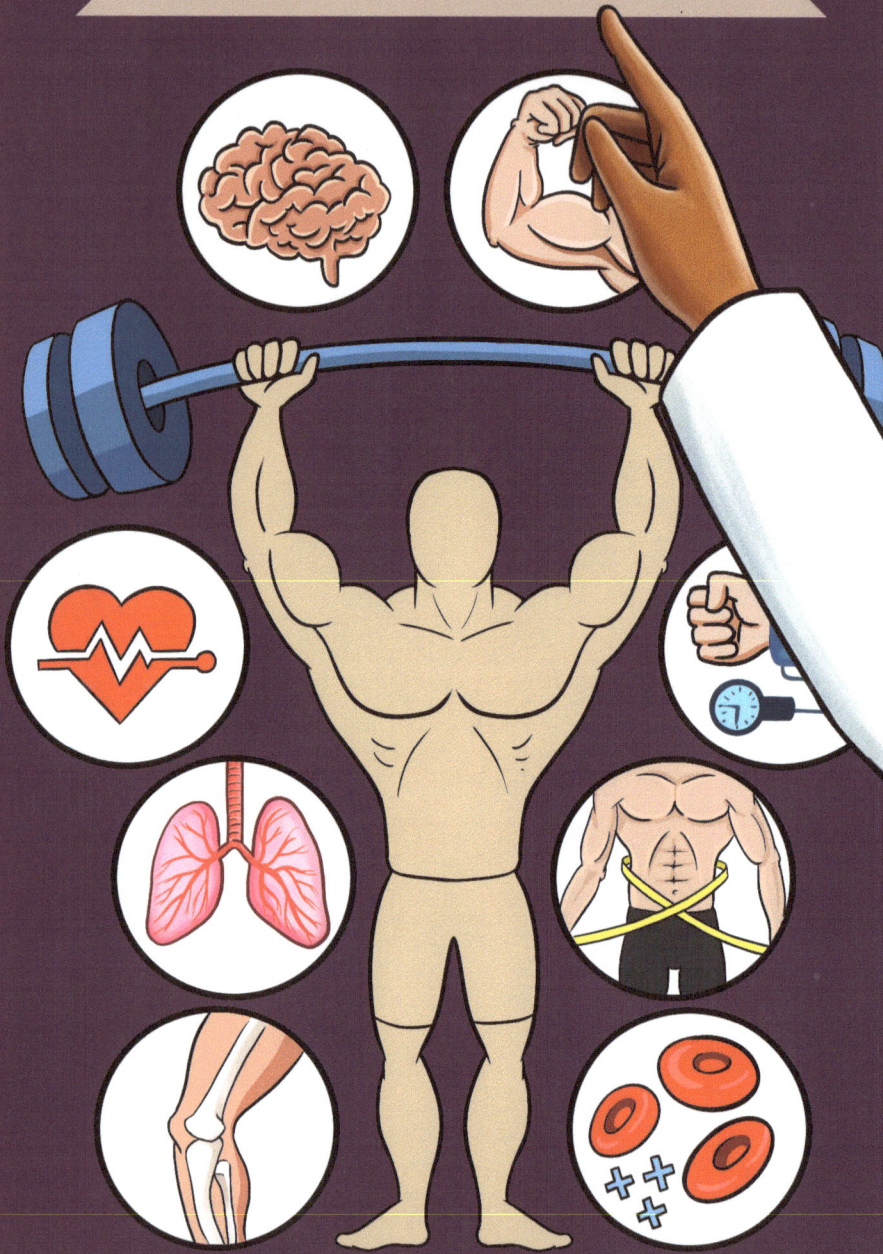

BENEFITS OF EXERCISE

"There are so many health benefits from regular physical exercise, such as weight reduction, building strong and healthy bones, lowering blood sugar, lowering blood pressure, and keeping you feeling happier. I want you to promise me that you'll visit Exo City daily," said Dr. Cooper.

"Hey, Dr. Cooper, I'm already feeling better. My headache is gone and I'm feeling better just from coming along with you on this journey," said Charlie.

"Choo choo! This strain is approaching Station Y. Y is for Yielding Years of abundant life. Charlie, I'm so happy that you came with me on this journey. Let's review some of the things you've learnt," said Dr. Cooper.

"Remember, we went to station G for Goals and you said you wanted to feel well again. Then we went out into the Environment and you enjoyed meeting Darling Sunshine."

"You got some vitamin D and you met Mr. Fresh Air and received some oxygen. Oxygen is good for your health."

"We discussed the importance of Timely Rest, and how the body heals and repairs cells and tissue during sleep."

"From there we visited Greenville where you met all these wonderful fruits and vegetables and learnt about all the health benefits they provide," said Dr. Cooper.

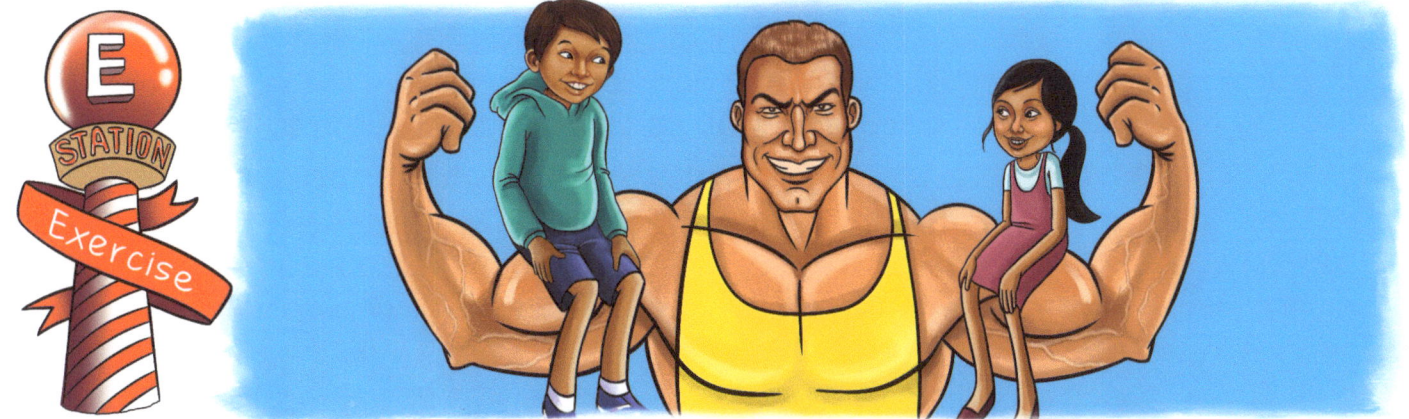

"Next we went through EXO City where you got to move your muscles and joints and have fun with Mr. Muscle Man."

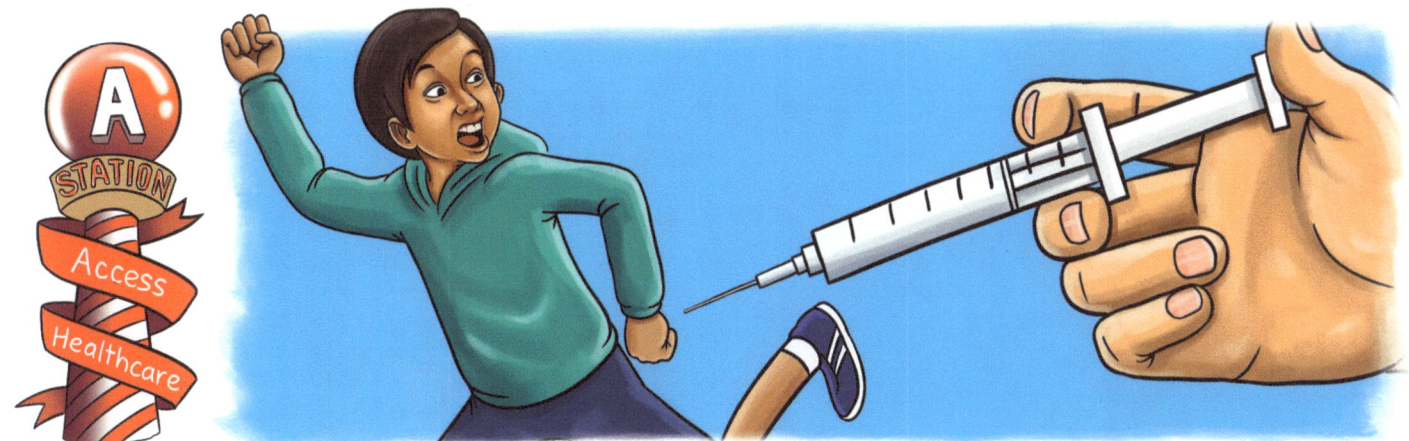

"Access is where you were so afraid of those needles, but there you got vital information which is so important for your health."

"And from there you got so thirsty that we had to go over to Station L for Liquid where you got the most important liquid for health, and that is water."

"It was a joy to watch you spending time with your new friend Annie. You were kind, caring and loving."

"Charlie you did so great on this trip, you brought hope and happiness to Annie's life. Great job!"

"Hey Charlie the secrets learned on this amazing train ride will Yield Years of a long, happy and healthy life." said Dr. Cooper.

"Charlie, it's now time to speak with your mom and I have your prescription ready. Hello, mom, Charlie had a wonderful ride on the GETHEALTHY train. I'm sure he'll tell you all about his experience. I have his prescription ready:"

Cooper Internal Medicine

Dona E Cooper-Dockery. MD. PA.

Name: Charlie Garcia   Date: 6/9/21

Adress:

Rx

Healthy Nutrition.

Fruit: a variety of fresh fruits daily.

Vegetables: a variety of fresh and steamed vegetables daily

Grains: wholegrains daily

Protein: legumes, soy product, nuts, seeds, or other healthy low-fat proteins.

Limit added sugar, saturated and trans fats.

Physical Exercise: 60 minutes daily for children under 18.

Sleep: seven to nine hours nightly.

Stress Management: 24 hours in an emotionally healthy environment that fosters healthy relationships, trust, happiness, and a positive mindset.

Charlie should have a dose of the above once daily for the rest of his life.

Dona E. Cooper-Dockery, M.D., P.A.

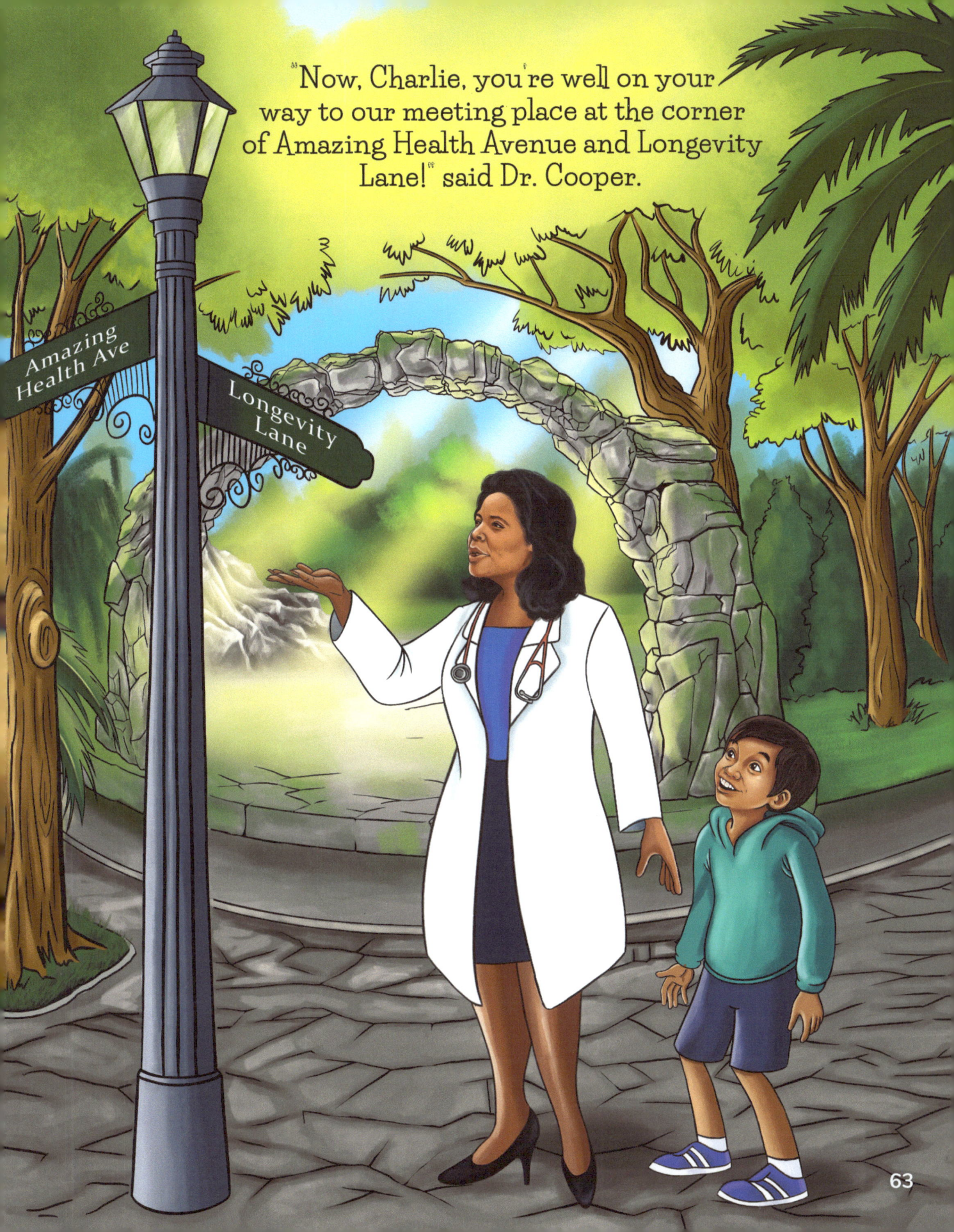

"Now, Charlie, you're well on your way to our meeting place at the corner of Amazing Health Avenue and Longevity Lane!" said Dr. Cooper.

CREATIVE WRITING
Create a story about the picture
Include the nutritive value of three of the fruits and two of the vegetables

_____
_____
_____
_____
_____
_____
_____
_____
_____
_____
_____
_____
_____
_____
_____
_____
_____

Healthy Foods Puzzle

1. Blueberry
2. Banana
3. Sweet potato
4. Lentil
5. Walnut
6. Raspberry
7. Lima bean
8. Kidney bean
9. Beet
10. Cashew
11. Peanut
12. Grape
13. Carrot
14. Kale
15. Orange
16. Grains
17. Almond
18. Pecan
19. Oats
20. Apple
21. Quinoa
22. Strawberry

```
R  T  U  B  Z  S  W  A  L  N  U  T  S  S
A  U  R  E  M  N  U  T  F  E  R  I  T  W
S  W  E  A  T  I  K  E  P  Q  S  M  R  E
P  L  T  I  Z  A  O  A  H  U  D  A  A  E
B  T  R  L  U  R  R  W  K  I  N  B  W  T
E  O  N  K  N  G  A  T  Y  N  O  E  B  P
R  R  Y  Y  P  T  N  R  W  O  M  A  E  O
R  R  A  I  D  L  G  Y  R  A  L  N  R  T
Y  A  K  S  D  N  E  K  B  E  A  O  R  A
L  C  A  T  H  E  W  A  H  X  P  J  Y  T
E  K  Y  E  T  M  N  U  C  E  P  E  T  O
A  A  L  X  N  K  O  L  K  A  L  P  U  A
A  B  E  N  R  T  T  U  A  N  E  I  L  S
J  B  A  U  E  B  E  E  R  R  Y  J  L  T
```

Help Charlie to choose healthy food

Put a check mark inside the circle next to each healthy meal.

Did you know?

Sugary drinks have a lot of sugar. For example, one can of soda contains 15 teaspoons of sugar. That's s a lot of sugar and it's not good for your health.
You need to drink enough water for your size.

www.ingramcontent.com/pod-product-compliance
Lightning Source LLC
Chambersburg PA
CBHW061056090426
42742CB00002B/55